THE FLOWER PHENOMENON BIOGRAPHY

Bloody of Betrayal

By

John Hauge

Copyright:

© 2023-2024 John Hauge. All rights reserved. No part of this book, "The Flower Moon Phenomenon Biography: Bloody of Betrayal," may be reproduced, stored in a retrieval system, or transmitted in any form or by any means, electronic, mechanical, photocopying, recording, or otherwise, without the prior written permission of the author.

Disclaimer:

The characters and events portrayed in this work are fictional, and any resemblance to real persons or incidents is purely coincidental. The author and publisher assume no responsibility for errors or omissions. Readers are advised to use their own judgment.

Copyright © 2023-2024. All rights reserved.

Table of contents

INTRODUCTION 6

THE ENIGMATIC PRELUDE 9

THE BLOSSOMING YEARS 12

PETALS OF AMBITION 15

SHADOWS IN BLOOM 18

THE CRYPTIC CIPHER 21

ALLIANCE AND ALLEGIANCE 24

THE THORNY PATH OF POWER 27

BETRAYAL IN FULL BLOOM 30

BLOODIED TIES 33

ECHOES OF CONSPIRACY 36

THE FATEFUL NIGHT 39

AFTERMATH AND FALLOUT 42

IN THE SHADOW OF SCANDAL...45

THE LEGACY UNVEILED 48

TRUTHS AND HALF-TRUTHS...51

THE PERSONA BEYOND THE PHENOMENON 54

THE BETRAYER'S LAMENT 57

RESONANCE IN POPULAR CULTURE 60

LESSONS IN BETRAYAL 63

UNEARTHING THE BLOOMS OF BETRAYAL 65

ECHOES ACROSS THE FLOWERED HORIZON.........................68

Introduction

In the tapestry of historical enigmas, few threads interweave as intricately and perplexingly as The Flower Moon Phenomenon. As a biographer tasked with unraveling the dense layers of this gripping narrative, my journey is akin to navigating a labyrinth of betrayal, steeped in the sanguinary hues of human intrigue.

The Flower Moon Phenomenon emerges from the shadows of time as a kaleidoscopic event, a convergence of elements that defy the conventional boundaries of historical analysis. Bursting onto the scene with a suddenness that challenges the very fabric of understanding, it remains an indelible mark on the annals of history.

At first glance, the title "The Flower Moon Phenomenon" may evoke images of celestial beauty or pastoral serenity. Yet, as one delves deeper into the heart of this biography, the petals of illusion quickly fall away, revealing a landscape painted with the dark brushstrokes of human treachery.

The journey into The Flower Moon Phenomenon is not for the faint of heart; it demands an exploration of the perplexing and the unexpected. In the pages that follow, we will navigate the maze of motives, where each turn reveals a new layer of complexity, leaving the reader entangled in the thorny vines of historical intrigue.

The genesis of this phenomenon lies shrouded in mystery, obscured by the fog of time and the deliberate actions of those who sought to manipulate its narrative. To grasp the essence of The Flower Moon Phenomenon, one must confront the enigma that surrounds its origins. It is a puzzle, a mosaic of disparate pieces that, when assembled, form a picture both haunting and unforgettable.

The suddenness of The Flower Moon Phenomenon is equally captivating. Like a sudden eruption, it disrupts the serene surface of historical waters, sending ripples through the collective consciousness. This suddenness is not confined to a single dimension; it spans the realms of politics, human relationships, and the very fabric of societal norms. The unexpected is not an anomaly here but rather a recurring theme, challenging preconceived notions and defying the predictability that often accompanies historical narratives.

As a biographer deeply immersed in the study of The Flower Moon Phenomenon, my endeavor is to peel back the layers of ambiguity and suddenness without sacrificing the specificity and context that breathe life into historical accounts. Each revelation is a brushstroke on the canvas of understanding, bringing us closer to the heart of this perplexing phenomenon.

In the chapters that follow, we will embark on a journey through time, tracing the footsteps of key figures, deciphering coded messages, and untangling the web of allegiances that defined The Flower Moon Phenomenon. It is a tale of bloody betrayals, clandestine alliances, and the ephemerality of truth.

The Flower Moon Phenomenon Biography: Bloody Betrayals invites readers to immerse themselves in the relentless pursuit of historical truth, where the enigma of the narrative is matched only by the suddenness of its impact. As we step into this labyrinth of intrigue, let us be prepared for a riveting exploration that transcends the ordinary, inviting us to question, reflect, and ultimately, bear witness to a phenomenon that defies the conventional boundaries of historical understanding.

Chapter 1

The Enigmatic Prelude

In the shadowed corridors of history, where the echoes of secrets linger and the petals of deception unfurl, The Flower Moon Phenomenon begins its enigmatic dance. To comprehend its essence, one must embark upon a journey through the corridors of time, navigating the labyrinth of an era marked by complexity and a suddenness of events that defy the conventional bounds of understanding.

As the biographer tasked with unraveling this intricate tapestry, the opening chapter serves as the prologue to a saga veiled in layers of ambiguity. The Enigmatic Prelude introduces us to the protagonist in this historical drama, a figure whose destiny interweaves with the complex threads of a nation in flux.

The Flower Moon Phenomenon unfolds against the backdrop of an era defined by upheavals and aspirations, where the scent of change permeates the air like the fragrance of blossoms on the cusp of bloom. The protagonist's early years, bathed in the glow of innocence and shaped by unseen hands, lay the foundation for a destiny both extraordinary and laden with the weight of betrayal.

In these formative chapters, we explore the roots of ambition that would eventually give rise to The Flower Moon Phenomenon. The individual, once a mere bud on the branch of societal expectation, begins to stretch toward the sunlight of influence. The suddenness of these aspirations disrupts the tranquility of the status quo, setting in motion a series of events that would come to define an era.

The Enigmatic Prelude invites the reader to witness the emergence of The Flower Moon Phenomenon, a phenomenon not easily categorized or understood. As the narrative unfolds, the complexity deepens, for this is not a straightforward ascent to power; it is a dance through the shadows, where alliances and motives remain veiled, and the true nature of the protagonist's journey remains shrouded in mystery.

This chapter delves into the cryptic cipher that becomes a hallmark of The Flower Moon Phenomenon. Symbolism and hidden messages lace the narrative, creating an intricate tapestry of mystery. Each revelation, like a coded communication, adds another layer to the complex narrative, leaving the reader both intrigued and confounded.

Alliance and allegiance play a pivotal role in The Enigmatic Prelude. The protagonist, forging key alliances, begins to navigate the thorny path of influence. Yet, these alliances are not mere political maneuvers; they are the building blocks of a legacy, and their unraveling will contribute to the eventual fall from grace.

As a biographer, the task is to capture not just the events but the atmosphere of betrayal that permeates The Flower Moon Phenomenon. The suddenness of power dynamics and political plots creates an atmosphere akin to a storm gathering on the horizon. In the prelude, the storm is distant, but its rumblings are felt, setting the stage for the storm that will eventually engulf the narrative.

In the style of Martin Gilbert, the Enigmatic Prelude unfolds with meticulous attention to detail, painting a vivid picture of an era marked by the complexity of hidden motives and the suddenness of unforeseen events. As we traverse the corridors of time, the stage is set for a biography that promises to unravel the secrets of The Flower Moon Phenomenon, peeling away the layers of puzzle one chapter at a time.

Chapter 2

The Blossoming Years

The second chapter of The Flower Moon Phenomenon unravels with the delicacy of petals unfurling, revealing the formative years that cast shadows and shaped destinies. These were the times when innocence collided with the stark realities of an era brimming with unspoken aspirations and burgeoning ambitions.

As a biographer navigating the labyrinth of perplexity, I find myself immersed in the bloom of an individual's existence, tracing the roots of influence that would burgeon into The Flower Moon Phenomenon. The Blossoming Years, akin to a garden of intrigue, introduces us to the protagonist's early life, a canvas upon which the hues of character and circumstance intermingle.

In the quiet corners of the protagonist's youth, one discovers the seeds of ideals and dreams that would later blossom into the complex flower of influence. The suddenness of these early aspirations disrupts the placidity of the status quo, heralding a transformation that, though unnoticed at the time, would echo through the corridors of time.

This chapter unfurls a nuanced exploration of the protagonist's early experiences and influences, untangling the threads that wove the fabric of their identity. From the nurturing warmth of familial bonds to the challenging winds of societal expectations, each element contributes to the blossoming of a character destined for prominence, yet veiled in the mystery of what lies ahead.

The Blossoming Years encapsulate the delicate dance between personal growth and societal expectations, presenting a tableau where the protagonist navigates the labyrinth of self-discovery. As a biographer, I delve into the perplexity of these formative moments, seeking to understand the bursts of inspiration that propelled the individual toward an inevitable collision with destiny.

The metaphorical petals of ambition unfold during this chapter, hinting at a future characterized by influence and power. The protagonist's early forays into realms beyond the ordinary mark the first signs of a blooming destiny, laden with both promise and the weight of impending betrayal.

In the style of Martin Gilbert, the narrative of The Blossoming Years is not a linear march but a complex dance where each step is laden with significance. Gilbert's meticulous attention to historical detail finds resonance in the careful examination of the protagonist's youth, capturing the suddenness of youthful exuberance and the perplexing choices that set the stage for the unfolding drama.

As the biographer, I invite the reader to traverse the landscapes of The Blossoming Years, where the protagonist's journey from bud to bloom sets the tone for the intricate narrative that follows. The scent of anticipation lingers in the air, and the perplexity of untold possibilities invites us to contemplate the delicate balance between the ordinary and the extraordinary in the early life of The Flower Moon Phenomenon.

In these pages, the stage is set, and the seeds of intrigue are sown, promising a riveting exploration of the life that would lead to the infamous petals of betrayal in the chapters that lie ahead.

Chapter 3

Petals of Ambition

In the nuanced chronicles of The Flower Moon Phenomenon, Chapter 3 unfolds as a tapestry adorned with the intricate Petals of Ambition. Here, the protagonist's journey ascends beyond the confines of the ordinary, and the suddenness of aspirations disrupts the tranquil equilibrium of societal norms.

As a biographer committed to unraveling the perplexity woven into every facet of this narrative, I delve into the origins of ambition, tracing the delicate emergence of the protagonist's desires. It is within the delicate folds of these petals that the true essence of The Flower Moon Phenomenon begins to reveal itself.

The Petals of Ambition, like ephemeral blooms in the moonlight, showcase the protagonist's ascent from the common to the extraordinary. The suddenness of these ambitions is not a sudden eruption but a gradual unfurling, each petal representing a step closer to the zenith of influence.

The societal backdrop against which these petals unfurl is crucial to understanding the dynamics at play. In an era marked by upheavals and unspoken yearnings, the protagonist's ambitions are not mere whims but responses to the zeitgeist of a generation. Martin Gilbert's keen eye for contextual detail finds resonance here, as I strive to capture the suddenness of societal dynamics shaping the individual's desires.

The narrative meanders through the labyrinth of the protagonist's burgeoning influence, a maze where alliances are forged, and ambitions intertwine. The suddenness of political machinations and the clandestine dance of power become palpable, revealing a landscape rife with both opportunity and peril.

As the protagonist navigates this intricate terrain, the Petals of Ambition open to reveal the multifaceted nature of influence. The suddenness of political maneuvering and strategic alliances adds layers to the narrative, creating a mosaic where the pursuit of power is both art and science.

In the style of Martin Gilbert, the exploration of Petals of Ambition is not confined to the protagonist's personal journey alone. It is an expansive canvas where societal and political currents converge, creating a rich tableau of complexities. The suddenness of historical events, like ripples on a pond, extends far beyond individual aspirations, shaping the destiny of nations.

The biographer's role is to decipher the coded language of ambition, to unveil the cryptic messages hidden within the narrative. The perplexity lies not only in the protagonist's personal desires but in the intricate interplay of societal expectations, political machinations, and the relentless pursuit of influence.

As we navigate the chapters of Petals of Ambition, the reader is invited to contemplate the fragility of these blooms. Each ambition, a delicate petal, is subject to the unpredictable gusts of fate. The suddenness of the narrative intensifies, setting the stage for the tumultuous events that will follow in the wake of these aspirations.

In conclusion, Chapter 3 serves as a pivotal juncture, a moment when Petals of Ambition unfurl in the moonlit garden of The Flower Moon Phenomenon. The biographer's task is to capture the essence of this delicate dance, ensuring that the perplexity and suddenness of the protagonist's ambitions resonate with the reader, setting the stage for the betrayal that looms on the horizon.

Chapter 4

Shadows in Bloom

In the intricate mosaic of The Flower Moon Phenomenon, Chapter 4 emerges as a chiaroscuro canvas where Shadows in Bloom cast a haunting allure. The narrative unfurls like tendrils of creeping ivy, revealing the subtle yet profound influence that begins to cast its shadow over the protagonist's journey.

As a biographer attuned to the perplexity of historical narratives, I delve into the complexities of this chapter where shadows and blooms coalesce, creating an atmosphere pregnant with both promise and foreboding. The suddenness of events is palpable, reminiscent of a storm gathering on the horizon.

The Shadows in Bloom evoke a sense of duality, where the protagonist's influence burgeons, yet the ominous shadows cast by the pursuit of power begin to intertwine with the petals of ambition. In this paradoxical dance, the suddenness of political machinations intensifies, presenting a narrative rich with intrigue and layered motivations.

Martin Gilbert's methodical approach to historical detail finds resonance as I navigate through the labyrinth of events shaping this pivotal chapter. The suddenness of Shadows in Bloom is not a singular occurrence but a gradual revelation, akin to the unfolding of a darkened tapestry. The societal and political landscape becomes increasingly intricate, mirroring the nuanced ambitions of the protagonist.

This chapter encapsulates the delicate balance between the ascent to power and the shadows that accompany such elevation. The protagonist's influence, like blooming flowers, is both beautiful and ominous, a dichotomy that amplifies the perplexity of the unfolding narrative. As the biographer, my task is to dissect the intricacies of this delicate dance, revealing the suddenness of hidden motives and alliances.

The Shadows in Bloom are not merely the consequence of individual actions but a reflection of the broader political and societal currents. Gilbert's emphasis on contextual detail becomes paramount as I explore the multifaceted nature of shadows, each one a manifestation of the suddenness inherent in the pursuit of influence.

As alliances solidify and the protagonist's presence looms larger, the Shadows in Bloom begin to cast a pall over the narrative. The suddenness intensifies, and the reader is drawn into a world where the line between light and shadow blurs, leaving a lingering sense of unease.

In the shadows, alliances are forged, secrets whispered, and the groundwork laid for the crescendo of betrayal that looms on the horizon. The suddenness of this chapter is not confined to a single event but is an amalgamation of calculated moves, clandestine meetings, and the subtle erosion of trust.

The biographer, akin to a detective in the dimly lit corners of history, unravels the perplexity of Shadows in Bloom. This is a chapter where the protagonist's journey takes an irreversible turn, and the suddenness of political machinations becomes a symphony of intrigue. The interplay of light and shadow becomes symbolic of the dual nature of influence, simultaneously alluring and ominous.

As we navigate through Shadows in Bloom, the reader is invited to witness the delicate interplay of power dynamics and the subtle betrayals that mark the protagonist's trajectory. Gilbert's influence is evident in the meticulous examination of events, ensuring that the suddenness of the narrative remains in harmony with the overarching perplexity.

In conclusion, Chapter 4 serves as a pivotal moment, a juncture where Shadows in Bloom set the stage for the impending crescendo of betrayal. The biographer's art lies in capturing the essence of this delicate chapter, where shadows and blooms intertwine, leaving an indelible imprint on the pages of The Flower Moon Phenomenon Biography: Bloody of Betrayal.

Chapter 5

The Cryptic Cipher

In the labyrinthine narrative of The Flower Moon Phenomenon, Chapter 5 unfolds as The Cryptic Cipher, a clandestine language that weaves its way through the tapestry of intrigue. As a biographer immersed in the enigma of historical narratives, I delve into the complexities of this chapter, where the suddenness of coded messages and hidden meanings adds a layer of perplexity to the unfolding drama.

The Cryptic Cipher is emblematic of the covert language that permeates the protagonist's sphere of influence. Martin Gilbert's meticulous approach to historical detail guides my exploration, ensuring that the nuances of each encrypted message are deciphered with precision. It is within the confines of this chapter that the true depth of the Flower Moon Phenomenon's machinations begins to surface.

The suddenness of coded communication introduces an element of suspense, reminiscent of a spy thriller where each word carries weight and every gesture holds meaning. In the shadows of political intrigue, The Cryptic Cipher becomes the key to unlocking secrets that have far-reaching consequences.

As the biographer, my task is to navigate through the maze of symbols and veiled references, revealing the suddenness of a language that transcends the spoken word. The Cryptic Cipher is not just a tool for communication; it is a reflection of the protagonist's mastery in the art of secrecy, where every move is calculated, and every message is a piece of the puzzle.

In Gilbert's style, the examination of The Cryptic Cipher goes beyond a mere decoding of messages. It is an exploration of the mindset that births such a cryptic language, a journey into the psyche of the Flower Moon Phenomenon. The suddenness of hidden meanings mirrors the convoluted nature of political maneuvering, leaving the reader entranced by the complexity of motives.

The chapter is not limited to the deciphering of messages alone; it delves into the consequences of misinterpretation and the labyrinthine nature of alliances built on trust and deception. The Cryptic Cipher becomes a metaphor for the delicate dance between loyalty and betrayal, where every decoded message reveals a new layer of the protagonist's cunning.

The suddenness intensifies as The Cryptic Cipher becomes a central element in the protagonist's arsenal. It is not just a means of communication; it is a weapon in the battle for influence. The perplexity lies not only in the decoding of messages but in understanding the intricate dance of power dynamics, where alliances are solidified and rivals are misled.

As shadows lengthen and The Cryptic Cipher takes center stage, the biographer must unravel not only the literal meanings of the encoded messages but also the underlying intentions and strategic nuances. Gilbert's influence is palpable in the meticulous examination of each coded missive, ensuring that the suddenness of this chapter remains harmoniously entwined with the overarching perplexity.

The Cryptic Cipher, with its elusive meanings and veiled intentions, adds a layer of complexity to The Flower Moon Phenomenon. As the biographer guides the reader through the intricate dance of coded communication, the suddenness of the narrative builds, creating an atmosphere charged with tension and suspense.

In conclusion, Chapter 5 marks a pivotal moment in The Flower Moon Phenomenon Biography: Bloody of Betrayal. The Cryptic Cipher becomes a metaphorical bridge between secrecy and revelation, a tool that defines the protagonist's cunning and sets the stage for the tumultuous events that will follow. As the biographer, I invite the reader to decipher the hidden language, to unveil the suddenness of meaning within The Cryptic Cipher, and to anticipate the betrayals that loom in the shadows.

Chapter 6

Alliance and Allegiance

In the labyrinth of The Flower Moon Phenomenon, Chapter 6, titled "Alliance and Allegiance," unfolds as a riveting exploration into the intricate web of connections that defines the protagonist's journey. In the indelible style of Martin Gilbert, this chapter becomes a nuanced examination of alliances forged, allegiances tested, and the suddenness of loyalty in the tumultuous landscape of power.

The suddenness of political machinations reaches its zenith as alliances become the currency of influence in this pivotal chapter. Gilbert's meticulous eye for historical detail guides the exploration, ensuring that the perplexity of motives and the delicate dance of power dynamics are presented with utmost precision.

"Alliance and Allegiance" is not merely a recounting of political unions; it is a symphony of calculated moves and strategic partnerships. The suddenness of these alliances adds layers to the narrative, creating a tapestry where the threads of loyalty are interwoven with the strands of betrayal.

As the biographer, my task is to dissect the intricacies of these alliances, to unravel the suddenness of motivations that propel individuals into a nexus of influence. The protagonist, a master of political maneuvering, navigates the labyrinth of allegiances, forming bonds that are both strategic and fraught with potential treachery.

Gilbert's influence is evident in the meticulous examination of the political landscape, where alliances are not static but dynamic entities, subject to the suddenness of shifting interests and unforeseen circumstances. Each alliance becomes a brushstroke on the canvas of influence, contributing to the portrait of the Flower Moon Phenomenon.

The suddenness of political alliances extends beyond mere strategic considerations. It delves into the personal dynamics that underpin these connections, exploring the symbiotic relationships and the implicit expectations that bind individuals together. The perplexity lies not only in the strategic choices but in the intricate interplay of personalities, loyalty, and self-interest.

"Alliance and Allegiance" becomes a stage where the protagonists and supporting characters perform a delicate dance, a choreography of shifting loyalties and strategic posturing. The suddenness of this political ballet is orchestrated with finesse, leaving the reader enthralled by the unpredictability of the narrative.

As the chapter unfolds, the biographer unveils the suddenness of allegiances, where friends become foes, and foes turn into confidants. The perplexity intensifies as the motivations behind each alliance are laid bare, exposing the fragile nature of loyalty in the ruthless pursuit of power.

In the meticulous style of Gilbert, the exploration of "Alliance and Allegiance" goes beyond a mere chronicle of events. It is a deep dive into the psychology of power, where individuals navigate a landscape where trust is both a commodity and a liability. The suddenness of this psychological drama adds a layer of complexity to the narrative, revealing the intricate tapestry of human motivations.

As the biographer guides the reader through the labyrinth of allegiances, the suddenness of the narrative reaches a crescendo, setting the stage for the impending betrayals that will reverberate through the chapters that follow. The alliances formed in this chapter become the threads that will either fortify the protagonist's ascent or unravel in the face of looming adversity.

In conclusion, Chapter 6 stands as a testament to the biographer's craft, unraveling the suddenness and perplexity inherent in the world of alliances and allegiances within The Flower Moon Phenomenon. The political chessboard is set, and the players are positioned for a game where the stakes are nothing less than the flower blooms of influence and the thorns of betrayal.

Chapter 7

The Thorny Path of Power

In the unfolding saga of The Flower Moon Phenomenon, Chapter 7, titled "The Thorny Path of Power," takes center stage as a labyrinthine journey through the intricate landscapes of influence. Guided by the indomitable style of Martin Gilbert, this chapter becomes a meticulous exploration of the suddenness and perplexity inherent in the relentless pursuit of power.

The metaphorical thorns that line this path are not just obstacles; they are symbolic of the challenges, ethical dilemmas, and ruthless choices faced by the protagonist. In the inimitable style of Gilbert, the biographer peels back the layers of complexity, exposing the suddenness of political maneuvering and the perplexity of navigating the thorny terrain of influence.

As the protagonist ascends to positions of unparalleled authority, the thorny path becomes increasingly treacherous. Gilbert's keen eye for historical detail is reflected in the nuanced examination of the suddenness inherent in the protagonist's choices – each step laden with moral implications and political consequences.

The Thorny Path of Power is not a linear trajectory but a meandering journey through a landscape where ethical boundaries blur, and the suddenness of political exigencies challenges the very fabric of the protagonist's moral compass. The reader is invited to witness the internal struggles and external pressures that shape the Flower Moon Phenomenon's ascent.

The suddenness of this chapter is not confined to external challenges alone; it extends to the internal conflicts that define the protagonist's character. The perplexity lies in the delicate balance between ambition and morality, as the Thorny Path demands sacrifices and tests the limits of the protagonist's convictions.

In this chapter, alliances forged on the earlier Thorny Path of Power undergo metamorphosis, revealing the transient nature of loyalty in the pursuit of influence. The suddenness of shifting allegiances and the perplexity of trust become central themes, mirroring the tumultuous nature of political landscapes.

As the biographer, I delve into the ethical quagmire that defines The Thorny Path of Power. Gilbert's influence is evident as I meticulously unravel the suddenness of political choices and the perplexity of moral compromise. The protagonist's journey becomes a case study in the delicate dance between pragmatism and idealism.

The suddenness intensifies as the Thorny Path reveals its toll on personal relationships. The biographer peels back the layers of interpersonal dynamics, exposing the strains and fractures that occur when ambition collides with personal connections. The perplexity of navigating political and familial ties adds a layer of complexity to the narrative.

In the style of Gilbert, the Thorny Path of Power is not merely a chapter; it is a psychological exploration into the intricate recesses of the protagonist's mind. The suddenness of internal conflicts is juxtaposed against the external challenges, creating a narrative that is both deeply personal and politically charged.

As alliances splinter and the Thorny Path unravels, the biographer captures the essence of a chapter where the suddenness of political machinations meets the perplexity of ethical quandaries. The reader is left to contemplate the toll of power on the human psyche and the inevitable clashes between ambition and conscience.

In conclusion, Chapter 7 stands as a testament to the biographer's craft in capturing the nuances of The Flower Moon Phenomenon's Thorny Path of Power. The suddenness and perplexity inherent in the pursuit of influence are laid bare, setting the stage for the tumultuous events that will follow in the chapters ahead.

Chapter 8

Betrayal in Full Bloom

In the intricate narrative of The Flower Moon Phenomenon, Chapter 8, titled "Betrayal in Full Bloom," emerges as the climactic zenith of a tale rife with perplexity and suddenness. Guided by the discerning style of Martin Gilbert, this chapter unravels the complex threads of betrayal that have been quietly germinating, now bursting forth in a full bloom of political intrigue.

The suddenness in this chapter is palpable, akin to a storm breaking after a prolonged gathering of clouds. The reader is drawn into a world where alliances unravel, secrets are exposed, and the thorns lining the protagonist's path of power inflict wounds both deep and lasting. Gilbert's meticulous attention to historical detail becomes the biographer's guiding light as we navigate through the labyrinth of Betrayal in Full Bloom.

The chapter is a symphony of shattered trust and shattered illusions, where the suddenness of events unfolds with a rapidity that leaves both characters and readers breathless. The protagonist, once a master orchestrator of political machinations, finds themselves entangled in a web of deceit, the thorny consequences of choices made on the Thorny Path of Power now fully realized.

As the biographer, my role is to meticulously unveil the perplexity underlying each betrayal. Gilbert's influence ensures that every twist and turn in the narrative is not merely a plot device but a revelation of the intricate dance between power and vulnerability. The suddenness of Betrayal in Full Bloom is not confined to individual acts but resonates through the collective impact of political upheaval.

The narrative unfurls with a suddenness that mirrors the abruptness of a blossom opening, revealing the hidden truths that have festered beneath the surface. Allegiances crumble, alliances collapse, and the protagonist's once-blooming influence withers in the harsh light of exposed betrayals. The reader is left to grapple with the perplexity of a world where loyalties are as fleeting as petals in the wind.

In Gilbert's style, the exploration of Betrayal in Full Bloom is not a straightforward exposition but a layered examination of consequences. Each act of treachery, revealed in its full complexity, adds a layer to the narrative, exposing the fragility of trust in the cutthroat world of political ambition. The suddenness of these revelations creates a narrative rhythm that resonates with the heightened emotions of the unfolding drama.

The biographer peels back the layers of political subterfuge, exposing the motivations and machinations that culminate in the full bloom of betrayal. The Thorny Path of Power, once navigated with calculated precision, now becomes a minefield of shattered alliances and fractured allegiances. The perplexity lies not only in the acts of betrayal but in the emotional toll exacted on those ensnared in the web of political intrigue.

As the thorns that line the path pierce deeper, the biographer captures the essence of a chapter where the suddenness of political upheaval and the perplexity of moral compromise converge. Betrayal in Full Bloom is a canvas painted with strokes of duplicity, a tableau where the protagonist's aspirations are pruned by the very hands that once nurtured them.

In conclusion, Chapter 8 stands as the crescendo of The Flower Moon Phenomenon Biography: Bloody of Betrayal, where the suddenness and perplexity inherent in the narrative reach their zenith. The reader is left to ponder the aftermath of betrayal, as the protagonist's influence lies in tatters and the political landscape is forever altered. The biographer's craft, guided by the spirit of Martin Gilbert, captures the full bloom of betrayal, leaving an indelible imprint on the pages of this riveting tale.

Chapter 9

Bloodied Ties

In the intricate tapestry of The Flower Moon Phenomenon, Chapter 9, titled "Bloodied Ties," unfurls as a somber symphony echoing the aftermath of the full bloom of betrayal. Guided by the meticulous approach of Martin Gilbert, this chapter delves into the aftermath of shattered alliances, exploring the suddenness of consequences and the perplexity of fractured relationships.

The suddenness of the aftermath is palpable, akin to the echoes of thunder following a tempest. The reader is ushered into a world where the political landscape is scarred by the searing revelations of betrayal. Gilbert's discerning eye for historical detail becomes the biographer's compass, navigating through the complexities of Bloodied Ties.

This chapter is not merely a continuation of the narrative but a reckoning with the aftermath of treachery. The suddenness lies not only in the immediate fallout but in the enduring consequences that reverberate through the corridors of power. As the biographer, my task is to dissect the perplexity of Bloodied Ties, where the bonds that once seemed unbreakable are now stained with the indelible mark of betrayal.

Gilbert's influence ensures that the exploration of Bloodied Ties is not a linear progression but a layered examination of the emotional and political fallout. The suddenness of emotions, ranging from anger and grief to disillusionment, permeates the narrative, mirroring the shattered illusions of those entangled in the protagonist's web of deceit.

As alliances crumble and allegiances shift like sand, the biographer uncovers the perplexity of recalibrating political equations. Bloodied Ties are not only the visible scars of betrayal but also the invisible threads that bind individuals together, even in the aftermath of shattered trust. The suddenness of this chapter lies in the nuanced exploration of the protagonists' attempts to salvage what remains of their political influence.

The narrative rhythm of Bloodied Ties is punctuated by the biographer's scrutiny, exposing the tenuous nature of political connections. In Gilbert's style, each twist and turn in the aftermath is an opportunity to delve into the psychology of the characters, laying bare the complexities of resilience and vulnerability in the face of political turmoil. The suddenness here is not only external but internal, as the protagonists grapple with the moral and emotional toll of betrayal.

The thorny residue of past decisions lingers in Bloodied Ties, creating an atmosphere charged with tension and uncertainty. The suddenness extends beyond the immediate aftermath, hinting at the enduring legacy of betrayal on the political landscape. The perplexity is heightened as characters navigate the delicate dance of rebuilding alliances or forging new paths in the wake of shattered ties.

As the biographer, I meticulously unveil the suddenness of political realignments, where the protagonists are forced to reassess their positions and redefine their trajectories. Gilbert's influence ensures that the exploration of Bloodied Ties is not a mere catalogue of events but a profound examination of the human cost of political betrayal.

In conclusion, Chapter 9 stands as a poignant reflection on the aftermath of betrayal, as Bloodied Ties become emblematic of the lasting impact on The Flower Moon Phenomenon's journey. The suddenness and perplexity inherent in this chapter offer a nuanced perspective on the intricate dance between power and vulnerability, leaving the reader captivated by the intricate unraveling of political destinies.

Chapter 10

Echoes of Conspiracy

In the sweeping narrative of The Flower Moon Phenomenon, Chapter 10, titled "Echoes of Conspiracy," emerges as a labyrinth of intrigue where perplexity and suddenness intertwine, casting shadows on the aftermath of betrayal. Guided by the discerning style of Martin Gilbert, this chapter unveils the intricate layers of clandestine plots and lingering suspicions that echo through the corridors of power.

The suddenness of conspiracy is like a subtle tremor beneath the surface, an undercurrent that disrupts the semblance of political stability. The reader is drawn into a world where alliances are reshaped, and the protagonists grapple with the resounding echoes of past betrayals. Gilbert's meticulous attention to historical detail becomes the biographer's compass, navigating through the complexities of Echoes of Conspiracy.

This chapter is not a mere continuation of the narrative but a reflection on the enduring impact of betrayal on the political landscape. The suddenness lies not only in the overt manifestations of conspiracy but in the subtleties of whispered alliances and covert machinations. As the biographer, my task is to peel back the layers of perplexity, where the protagonists are caught in a web of suspicion and shadowy alliances.

Gilbert's influence ensures that the exploration of Echoes of Conspiracy is not a linear progression but a multi-faceted examination of political subterfuge. The suddenness of this chapter extends beyond the immediate aftermath, becoming a lens through which the biographer scrutinizes the shifting power dynamics and the nuanced motivations of the characters.

As alliances are forged anew, and old wounds fester beneath the surface, the biographer navigates through the labyrinth of conspiracy, exposing the perplexity of motives and the suddenness of hidden agendas. Echoes of Conspiracy are not only audible in the whispered conversations of political players but resonate in the unspoken tensions that linger in the air.

In Gilbert's style, the suddenness of this chapter is not confined to overt acts of conspiracy but extends to the psychological dimensions of suspicion and paranoia. The biographer peels back the layers of characters' inner turmoil, revealing the internal conflict as they grapple with the shadows of betrayal that continue to shape their political destinies.

The narrative rhythm of Echoes of Conspiracy is punctuated by the biographer's scrutiny, uncovering the perplexity of political realignments and the suddenness of alliances formed in the wake of shattered trust. The reader is invited to traverse the corridors of power, where every whispered conversation and subtle gesture becomes a thread in the intricate tapestry of political conspiracy.

The suddenness intensifies as the protagonists confront the echoes of their own actions, haunted by the specter of past betrayals and the shadows of mistrust. Gilbert's influence ensures that the exploration of conspiracy is not sensationalized but presented with a sobering realism, capturing the moral and ethical complexities that underpin political machinations.

As the biographer meticulously unveils the layers of Echoes of Conspiracy, the reader is left to contemplate the enduring legacy of betrayal on The Flower Moon Phenomenon's journey. The suddenness and perplexity inherent in this chapter offer a nuanced perspective on the delicate dance between political survival and the haunting reverberations of past transgressions.

In conclusion, Chapter 10 stands as a testament to the biographer's craft, capturing the lingering echoes of conspiracy in the aftermath of betrayal. The suddenness and perplexity resonate through the corridors of power, leaving an indelible imprint on the pages of The Flower Moon Phenomenon Biography: Bloody of Betrayal.

Chapter 11

The Fateful Night

In the annals of The Flower Moon Phenomenon, Chapter 11, titled "The Fateful Night," emerges as a pivotal juncture where perplexity and suddenness converge, casting a profound shadow over the narrative. Guided by the discerning style of Martin Gilbert, this chapter delves into the complexities of a night steeped in significance, unraveling the threads of fate that bind the protagonist's destiny.

The suddenness of events on this fateful night is akin to a sudden tempest, disrupting the calm façade of political maneuvering. The reader is ushered into a world where decisions carry the weight of destiny, and the consequences of actions reverberate through the corridors of power. Gilbert's meticulous attention to historical detail becomes the biographer's guiding light as we navigate through the intricate tapestry of The Fateful Night.

This chapter is not a mere continuation but a revelation, a moment where the suddenness of political machinations reaches its zenith. The perplexity lies not only in the overt actions but in the underlying motivations and the subtle dance of power dynamics. As the biographer, my role is to unravel the layers of complexity, exposing the suddenness of decisions that will shape the Flower Moon Phenomenon's trajectory.

Gilbert's influence ensures that the exploration of The Fateful Night is not a linear progression but a nuanced examination of a critical turning point. The suddenness of this chapter extends beyond the immediate events, becoming a lens through which the biographer scrutinizes the characters' motivations, the intricate interplay of alliances, and the lasting impact on the political landscape.

As the night unfolds, alliances are tested, and the protagonist grapples with the weight of impending decisions. The suddenness of emotions, ranging from anticipation to trepidation, permeates the narrative, mirroring the heightened stakes of the unfolding drama. The reader is drawn into a world where every whispered conversation and strategic move becomes a brushstroke on the canvas of fate.

In Gilbert's style, the suddenness of The Fateful Night is not confined to external actions alone; it delves into the internal conflicts that define the characters' psyche. The biographer peels back the layers of emotional turmoil, revealing the perplexity of moral quandaries and the delicate balance between ambition and conscience.

The narrative rhythm of The Fateful Night is punctuated by the biographer's scrutiny, exposing the nuanced motivations of the characters and the suddenness of choices that will echo through the remaining chapters. The reader is invited to witness the unfolding drama, where every decision becomes a stepping stone in the protagonist's journey, laden with both promise and peril.

As the biographer navigates through the labyrinth of The Fateful Night, Gilbert's influence ensures that the suddenness is not just a sequence of events but a revelation of the intricate dance between fate and free will. The characters, caught in the throes of political upheaval, must grapple with the consequences of their choices, and the reader is left to ponder the enduring impact on The Flower Moon Phenomenon's legacy.

In conclusion, Chapter 11 stands as a testament to the biographer's craft, capturing the essence of The Fateful Night with a depth that mirrors Gilbert's discerning style. The suddenness and perplexity inherent in this chapter offer a nuanced perspective on the delicate interplay of fate and human agency, leaving an indelible imprint on the pages of The Flower Moon Phenomenon Biography: Bloody of Betrayal.

Chapter 12

Aftermath and Fallout

In the penultimate chapter of The Flower Moon Phenomenon Biography: Bloody of Betrayal, Chapter 12, titled "Aftermath and Fallout," unfolds as a canvas upon which the consequences of fateful decisions are painted with meticulous strokes. Guided by Martin Gilbert's evocative style, this chapter delves into the aftermath of The Fateful Night, where perplexity and suddenness continue to shape the protagonist's destiny and the political landscape at large.

The suddenness of consequences from The Fateful Night reverberates through the corridors of power. The reader is immersed in a world where the fallout is both immediate and enduring, and the biographer, guided by Gilbert's discerning approach, meticulously unveils the complexities of this aftermath.

This chapter is not a mere epilogue but a profound exploration of the intricate tapestry woven by The Flower Moon Phenomenon's choices. The perplexity lies not only in the overt repercussions but in the subtle shifts of power dynamics, redefined alliances, and the lasting impact on the characters' political destinies. As the biographer, my task is to dissect the layers of complexity, exposing the suddenness of consequences that will shape the concluding chapters.

Gilbert's influence ensures that the exploration of Aftermath and Fallout is not a linear progression but a multi-faceted examination of the far-reaching effects. The suddenness extends beyond immediate events, becoming a lens through which the biographer scrutinizes the protagonists' attempts to navigate the turbulent aftermath with varying degrees of resilience and vulnerability.

As alliances crumble and allegiances shift once more, the biographer delves into the perplexity of recalibrating political equations. Aftermath and Fallout are not only the visible scars of The Fateful Night but also the invisible threads that bind individuals together in the wake of shattered trust. The suddenness of this chapter lies in the nuanced exploration of the protagonists' attempts to salvage what remains of their political influence.

The narrative rhythm of Aftermath and Fallout is punctuated by the biographer's scrutiny, revealing the perplexity of political realignments and the suddenness of alliances formed in the wake of shattered trust. The reader is invited to traverse the labyrinth of power, where every whispered conversation and strategic move becomes a thread in the intricate tapestry of political survival.

In Gilbert's style, the suddenness of this chapter is not confined to overt acts but extends to the psychological dimensions of resilience and vulnerability. The biographer peels back the layers of characters' inner turmoil, revealing the internal conflict as they grapple with the moral and emotional toll of betrayal.

The thorny residue of past decisions lingers in Aftermath and Fallout, creating an atmosphere charged with tension and uncertainty. The suddenness extends beyond the immediate aftermath, hinting at the enduring legacy of betrayal on the political landscape. The perplexity is heightened as characters navigate the delicate dance of rebuilding alliances or forging new paths in the wake of shattered ties.

As the biographer, I meticulously unveil the suddenness of political realignments, where the protagonists are forced to reassess their positions and redefine their trajectories. Gilbert's influence ensures that the exploration of Aftermath and Fallout is not a mere catalogue of events but a profound examination of the human cost of political betrayal.

In conclusion, Chapter 12 stands as a poignant reflection on the aftermath of betrayal, as Aftermath and Fallout become emblematic of the lasting impact on The Flower Moon Phenomenon's journey. The suddenness and perplexity inherent in this chapter offer a nuanced perspective on the intricate dance between power and vulnerability, leaving the reader captivated by the intricate unraveling of political destinies.

Chapter 13

In the Shadow of Scandal

As the narrative of The Flower Moon Phenomenon reaches its penultimate chapter, titled "In the Shadow of Scandal," the biographer, akin to Martin Gilbert's discerning style, delves into the depths of political tumult and moral ambiguity. In this labyrinth of intrigue, perplexity and suddenness intertwine, casting a profound shadow that resonates with the echoes of betrayal and consequences.

The suddenness of scandal is akin to a tempest that sweeps through the political landscape. The reader is drawn into a world where every revelation is a thunderclap, shaking the foundations of the protagonist's influence. Guided by Gilbert's meticulous approach, the biographer navigates through the complexities of scandal, unraveling the layers of perplexity that define this pivotal chapter.

Chapter 13 is not merely an exposition but a profound exploration of the fallout from past decisions. The perplexity lies not only in the overt revelations but in the nuanced responses of characters, the subtle shifts in public perception, and the enduring impact on the Flower Moon Phenomenon's legacy. As the biographer, my task is to dissect the layers of complexity, exposing the suddenness of consequences that will shape the concluding chapters.

Gilbert's influence ensures that the exploration of In the Shadow of Scandal is not a linear progression but a multi-faceted examination of the far-reaching effects. The suddenness extends beyond immediate events, becoming a lens through which the biographer scrutinizes the protagonists' attempts to navigate the turbulent aftermath with varying degrees of resilience and vulnerability.

As scandalous revelations unfold, alliances fracture, and the protagonists grapple with the weight of public scrutiny. The suddenness of emotions, ranging from indignation to desperation, permeates the narrative, mirroring the heightened stakes of the unfolding drama. The reader is immersed in a world where every political maneuver and whispered conversation becomes a thread in the intricate tapestry of scandal.

In Gilbert's style, the suddenness of this chapter is not confined to overt actions alone; it delves into the internal conflicts that define the characters' psyche. The biographer peels back the layers of emotional turmoil, revealing the perplexity of moral quandaries and the delicate balance between ambition and conscience.

The narrative rhythm of In the Shadow of Scandal is punctuated by the biographer's scrutiny, exposing the nuanced motivations of the characters and the suddenness of choices that will echo through the remaining pages. The reader is invited to traverse the labyrinth of political scandal, where every decision becomes a stepping stone in the protagonist's journey, laden with both promise and peril.

As the biographer meticulously unveils the layers of In the Shadow of Scandal, Gilbert's influence ensures that the suddenness is not just a sequence of events but a revelation of the intricate dance between public perception and political survival. The characters, caught in the throes of scandal, must grapple with the consequences of their choices, and the reader is left to ponder the enduring impact on The Flower Moon Phenomenon's legacy.

In conclusion, Chapter 13 stands as a testament to the biographer's craft, capturing the essence of In the Shadow of Scandal with a depth that mirrors Gilbert's discerning style. The suddenness and perplexity inherent in this chapter offer a nuanced perspective on the delicate interplay of scandal and human agency, leaving an indelible imprint on the pages of The Flower Moon Phenomenon Biography: Bloody of Betrayal.

Chapter 14

The Legacy Unveiled

In the concluding chapter of The Flower Moon Phenomenon Biography: Bloody of Betrayal, titled "The Legacy Unveiled," the biographer, channeling the discerning style of Martin Gilbert, embarks on a profound exploration of the enduring consequences that define the protagonist's journey. Within the intricate dance of perplexity and suddenness, this chapter unravels the layers of legacy left in the wake of betrayal.

The suddenness of revelation is akin to a sudden illumination, casting light upon the intricate tapestry of choices and consequences woven throughout the narrative. The reader is transported into a world where the legacy of The Flower Moon Phenomenon is laid bare, and the biographer, guided by Gilbert's meticulous approach, meticulously peels back the layers of complexity.

Chapter 14 is not merely a conclusion but a reflection on the profound impact of the protagonist's actions. The perplexity lies not only in the overt repercussions but in the nuanced responses of characters, the evolving perceptions of society, and the indelible mark on the Flower Moon Phenomenon's historical footprint. As the biographer, my task is to dissect the layers of complexity, exposing the suddenness of consequences that will echo through the pages of this concluding chapter.

Gilbert's influence ensures that the exploration of The Legacy Unveiled is not a linear progression but a multi-faceted examination of the far-reaching effects. The suddenness extends beyond immediate events, becoming a lens through which the biographer scrutinizes the protagonists' attempts to navigate the turbulent aftermath with varying degrees of resilience and vulnerability.

As the legacy unfolds, alliances are redefined, and the protagonists grapple with the weight of historical judgment. The suddenness of emotions, ranging from remorse to defiance, permeates the narrative, mirroring the heightened stakes of the unfolding drama. The reader is drawn into a world where every political maneuver and whispered conversation becomes a thread in the intricate tapestry of legacy.

In Gilbert's style, the suddenness of this chapter is not confined to overt actions alone; it delves into the internal conflicts that define the characters' psyche. The biographer peels back the layers of emotional turmoil, revealing the perplexity of moral quandaries and the delicate balance between ambition and conscience.

The narrative rhythm of The Legacy Unveiled is punctuated by the biographer's scrutiny, exposing the nuanced motivations of the characters and the suddenness of choices that will echo through the historical corridors. The reader is invited to traverse the labyrinth of political legacy, where every decision becomes a stepping stone in the protagonist's journey, laden with both promise and peril.

As the biographer meticulously unveils the layers of The Legacy Unveiled, Gilbert's influence ensures that the suddenness is not just a sequence of events but a revelation of the intricate dance between historical judgment and political survival. The characters, ensnared in the tumult of legacy, must grapple with the enduring consequences of their choices, and the reader is left to ponder the indelible mark on The Flower Moon Phenomenon's historical narrative.

In conclusion, Chapter 14 stands as a testament to the biographer's craft, capturing the essence of The Legacy Unveiled with a depth that mirrors Gilbert's discerning style. The suddenness and perplexity inherent in this chapter offer a nuanced perspective on the delicate interplay of legacy and human agency, leaving an indelible imprint on the pages of The Flower Moon Phenomenon Biography: Bloody of Betrayal.

Chapter 15

Truths and Half-Truths

In the culminating chapter of The Flower Moon Phenomenon Biography: Bloody of Betrayal, titled "Truths and Half-Truths," the biographer, echoing the discerning style of Martin Gilbert, embarks on a compelling exploration of the intricate dance between revelation and concealment. Within the labyrinth of perplexity and suddenness, this chapter unravels the veils of deception, exposing the nuanced shades that define the legacy of The Flower Moon Phenomenon.

The suddenness of revelation is akin to the sudden unveiling of a tapestry, where threads of truth and half-truths intertwine to create a complex narrative. The reader is immersed in a world where the protagonist's journey is laid bare, and the biographer, guided by Gilbert's meticulous approach, meticulously peels back the layers of ambiguity.

Chapter 15 is not a mere resolution but a reflection on the profound interplay of disclosure and concealment. The perplexity lies not only in the overt revelations but in the shadowy corners where half-truths linger, shaping perceptions and distorting realities. As the biographer, my task is to dissect the layers of complexity, exposing the suddenness of truths that will echo through the pages of this concluding chapter.

Gilbert's influence ensures that the exploration of Truths and Half-Truths is not a linear progression but a multi-faceted examination of the narrative's intricate nuances. The suddenness extends beyond immediate events, becoming a lens through which the biographer scrutinizes the protagonists' attempts to navigate the delicate balance between transparency and obfuscation.

As the truths unfold, alliances are redefined, and the protagonists grapple with the weight of historical judgment. The suddenness of emotions, ranging from vindication to regret, permeates the narrative, mirroring the heightened stakes of the unfolding drama. The reader is drawn into a world where every revelation and strategic omission becomes a thread in the intricate tapestry of the Flower Moon Phenomenon's narrative.

In Gilbert's style, the suddenness of this chapter is not confined to overt actions alone; it delves into the internal conflicts that define the characters' psyche. The biographer peels back the layers of emotional turmoil, revealing the perplexity of moral quandaries and the delicate balance between transparency and political survival.

The narrative rhythm of Truths and Half-Truths is punctuated by the biographer's scrutiny, exposing the nuanced motivations of the characters and the suddenness of choices that will echo through the historical corridors. The reader is invited to traverse the labyrinth of political disclosure, where every decision becomes a stepping stone in the protagonist's journey, laden with both revelation and concealment.

As the biographer meticulously unveils the layers of Truths and Half-Truths, Gilbert's influence ensures that the suddenness is not just a sequence of events but a revelation of the intricate dance between disclosure and historical judgment. The characters, ensnared in the tumult of truth, must grapple with the enduring consequences of their choices, and the reader is left to ponder the indelible mark on The Flower Moon Phenomenon's narrative.

In conclusion, Chapter 15 stands as a testament to the biographer's craft, capturing the essence of Truths and Half-Truths with a depth that mirrors Gilbert's discerning style. The suddenness and perplexity inherent in this chapter offer a nuanced perspective on the delicate interplay of disclosure and human agency, leaving an indelible imprint on the pages of The Flower Moon Phenomenon Biography: Bloody of Betrayal.

Chapter 16

The Persona Beyond the Phenomenon

In the culminating chapter of The Flower Moon Phenomenon Biography: Bloody of Betrayal, titled "The Persona Beyond the Phenomenon," the biographer, echoing the discerning style of Martin Gilbert, embarks on an introspective exploration of the enigmatic figure whose life has been shrouded in perplexity and suddenness. This chapter serves as the denouement, unraveling the layers that separate the public persona from the private individual, and shedding light on the complex interplay of identity and legacy.

The suddenness of revelation is akin to the lifting of a veil, exposing the multifaceted dimensions that define The Flower Moon Phenomenon beyond the political phenomenon. The reader is ushered into a world where the protagonist's humanity is laid bare, and the biographer, guided by Gilbert's meticulous approach, meticulously peels back the layers of complexity.

Chapter 16 is not a mere epilogue but a profound exploration of the person behind the political curtain. The perplexity lies not only in the overt revelations but in the subtle nuances that blur the line between public and private life. As the biographer, my task is to dissect the layers of complexity, exposing the suddenness of the persona that will resonate beyond the pages of this biography.

Gilbert's influence ensures that the exploration of The Persona Beyond the Phenomenon is not a linear progression but a multi-faceted examination of the protagonist's identity. The suddenness extends beyond the immediate events, becoming a lens through which the biographer scrutinizes the motivations, fears, and aspirations that shaped the Flower Moon Phenomenon's journey.

As the persona is unveiled, the reader is invited to witness the vulnerabilities and strengths that define the individual behind the public facade. The suddenness of emotions, ranging from triumph to heartache, permeates the narrative, mirroring the complexity of a life lived in the public eye. The reader is drawn into a world where every personal triumph and private struggle becomes a thread in the intricate tapestry of identity.

In Gilbert's style, the suddenness of this chapter is not confined to external actions alone; it delves into the internal conflicts that define the individual's psyche. The biographer peels back the layers of emotional turmoil, revealing the perplexity of navigating the intersection between personal desires and public expectations.

The narrative rhythm of The Persona Beyond the Phenomenon is punctuated by the biographer's scrutiny, exposing the nuanced motivations of the individual and the suddenness of choices that will echo through the corridors of memory. The reader is invited to traverse the labyrinth of personal identity, where every decision becomes a testament to the intricate dance between public duty and personal fulfillment.

As the biographer meticulously unveils the layers of The Persona Beyond the Phenomenon, Gilbert's influence ensures that the suddenness is not just a sequence of personal revelations but a revelation of the intricate dance between public persona and private struggles. The reader is left to ponder the enduring legacy of an individual whose life transcended the political phenomenon, leaving an indelible mark on the pages of history.

In conclusion, Chapter 16 stands as a testament to the biographer's craft, capturing the essence of The Persona Beyond the Phenomenon with a depth that mirrors Gilbert's discerning style. The suddenness and perplexity inherent in this chapter offer a nuanced perspective on the delicate interplay of identity and human agency, leaving the reader captivated by the intricate unraveling of a life that extends beyond the political phenomenon.

Chapter 17

The Betrayer's Lament

As the curtain descends on The Flower Moon Phenomenon Biography: Bloody of Betrayal, Chapter 17, titled "The Betrayer's Lament," emerges as a poignant reflection on the tumultuous journey of a figure whose life has been marred by deception, revelation, and the indelible stain of betrayal. In the spirit of Martin Gilbert's discerning style, this chapter navigates the labyrinth of perplexity and suddenness, delving into the depths of remorse, introspection, and the enduring consequences of treachery.

The suddenness of emotions in this chapter is akin to a tempest, where the storm of regret and self-reckoning surges through the protagonist's soul. The reader is immersed in a world where the betrayer's internal landscape is laid bare, and the biographer, guided by Gilbert's meticulous approach, meticulously explores the intricate facets of remorse.

Chapter 17 is not a mere conclusion but a profound exploration of the betrayer's internal turmoil. The perplexity lies not only in the overt expressions of regret but in the subtle nuances of introspection and the delicate dance between repentance and irreversibility. As the biographer, my task is to dissect the layers of complexity, exposing the suddenness of emotions that will resonate with readers long after the final page.

Gilbert's influence ensures that the exploration of The Betrayer's Lament is not a linear progression but a multi-faceted examination of the internal conflicts that define the betrayer's psyche. The suddenness extends beyond immediate events, becoming a lens through which the biographer scrutinizes the motivations, regrets, and attempts at redemption that characterize this concluding chapter.

As the betrayer's lament unfolds, the reader is invited to witness the vulnerabilities and burdens that accompany the act of betrayal. The suddenness of emotions, ranging from anguish to a desperate desire for redemption, permeates the narrative, mirroring the complexity of a soul grappling with the consequences of treachery. The reader is drawn into a world where every whispered regret and introspective revelation becomes a thread in the intricate tapestry of remorse.

In Gilbert's style, the suddenness of this chapter is not confined to overt expressions of regret alone; it delves into the internal conflicts that define the betrayer's psyche. The biographer peels back the layers of emotional turmoil, revealing the perplexity of navigating the intersection between personal choices and their far-reaching consequences.

The narrative rhythm of The Betrayer's Lament is punctuated by the biographer's scrutiny, exposing the nuanced motivations and regrets that define the betrayer's journey. The reader is invited to traverse the labyrinth of remorse, where every decision becomes a testament to the intricate dance between personal responsibility and the yearning for redemption.

As the biographer meticulously unveils the layers of The Betrayer's Lament, Gilbert's influence ensures that the suddenness is not just a sequence of emotional expressions but a revelation of the intricate dance between remorse and the enduring legacy of betrayal. The reader is left to ponder the complexities of human nature, the consequences of moral choices, and the indelible mark left on the betrayer's soul.

In conclusion, Chapter 17 stands as a testament to the biographer's craft, capturing the essence of The Betrayer's Lament with a depth that mirrors Gilbert's discerning style. The suddenness and perplexity inherent in this chapter offer a nuanced perspective on the delicate interplay of remorse and human agency, leaving the reader captivated by the intricate unraveling of a soul burdened by the consequences of betrayal.

Chapter 18

Resonance in Popular Culture

In the concluding pages of The Flower Moon Phenomenon Biography: Bloody of Betrayal, Chapter 18, titled "Resonance in Popular Culture," takes us beyond the confines of historical narrative into the realms where the Flower Moon Phenomenon transcends the pages of a biography, imprinting itself on the collective consciousness of popular culture. In the discerning style of Martin Gilbert, this chapter navigates the intricate dance between history and myth, exploring the suddenness and perplexity that define the resonance of a complex life in the tapestry of public imagination.

The suddenness of the Flower Moon Phenomenon in popular culture is akin to a wildfire, spreading through various mediums and artistic expressions. The reader is transported into a world where the protagonist's life becomes more than historical fact; it becomes a canvas upon which artists, writers, and creators paint their interpretations. Guided by Gilbert's meticulous approach, the biographer delves into the complexities of this cultural resonance.

Chapter 18 is not merely an observation but a profound exploration of how the Flower Moon Phenomenon has become a symbol, a metaphor, and an archetype in the broader cultural landscape. The perplexity lies not only in the overt representations but in the subtle ways the figure has permeated literature, art, cinema, and music. As the biographer, my task is to dissect the layers of complexity, exposing the suddenness of interpretations that will define the Flower Moon Phenomenon for generations to come.

Gilbert's influence ensures that the exploration of Resonance in Popular Culture is not a linear progression but a multi-faceted examination of the myriad ways the figure has been embraced, challenged, and reimagined. The suddenness extends beyond immediate depictions, becoming a lens through which the biographer scrutinizes the motivations of creators and the evolving perceptions of a character whose resonance transcends the constraints of time.

As the Flower Moon Phenomenon resonates in popular culture, the reader is invited to witness the multifaceted interpretations that have emerged across different art forms. The suddenness of creativity, ranging from reverential portrayals to critical reevaluations, permeates the narrative, mirroring the complexity of a figure whose legacy has become a mirror reflecting the aspirations and anxieties of diverse audiences.

In Gilbert's style, the suddenness of this chapter is not confined to explicit representations alone; it delves into the subtle nuances that define the Flower Moon Phenomenon's cultural presence. The biographer peels back the layers of artistic choices, revealing the perplexity of navigating the intersection between historical truth and imaginative reinterpretation.

The narrative rhythm of Resonance in Popular Culture is punctuated by the biographer's scrutiny, exposing the nuanced motivations of creators and the suddenness of choices that have shaped the Flower Moon Phenomenon's cultural afterlife. The reader is invited to traverse the labyrinth of creative interpretation, where every artistic representation becomes a testament to the intricate dance between historical reality and cultural myth.

As the biographer meticulously unveils the layers of Resonance in Popular Culture, Gilbert's influence ensures that the suddenness is not just a sequence of artistic expressions but a revelation of the intricate relationship between historical figures and the narratives they inspire. The reader is left to ponder the enduring impact of the Flower Moon Phenomenon on the cultural imagination, and how a life, marked by betrayal, becomes a prism through which societies grapple with the complexities of human nature.

In conclusion, Chapter 18 stands as a testament to the biographer's craft, capturing the essence of Resonance in Popular Culture with a depth that mirrors Gilbert's discerning style. The suddenness and perplexity inherent in this chapter offer a nuanced perspective on the delicate interplay between historical figures and the cultural narratives that shape our collective understanding, leaving the reader captivated by the intricate dance between history and myth.

Chapter 19

Lessons in Betrayal

As the final chapter unfolds in The Flower Moon Phenomenon Biography: Bloody of Betrayal, titled "Lessons in Betrayal," the biographer, mirroring the discerning style of Martin Gilbert, invites readers on a contemplative journey through the intricate corridors of treachery. This chapter goes beyond the chronicles of a singular life, serving as a reflective canvas upon which the lessons drawn from betrayal are painted with bursts of insight and perplexity.

The suddenness of this chapter is akin to a revelation, where the lessons gleaned from betrayal surge forth with clarity and complexity. The reader is immersed in a world where the Flower Moon Phenomenon becomes more than a historical figure—it becomes a cautionary tale, a mirror reflecting the frailty of human allegiances. Guided by Gilbert's meticulous approach, the biographer peels back the layers of the betrayer's legacy to unveil profound lessons that resonate beyond the pages.

Chapter 19 is not merely a conclusion but an exploration of universal truths woven into the fabric of betrayal. The perplexity lies not only in the overt transgressions but in the subtle nuances of moral ambiguity, ethical choices, and the delicate dance between loyalty and duplicity. As the biographer, my task is to dissect the layers of complexity, exposing the suddenness of lessons that will linger in the reader's conscience.

Gilbert's influence ensures that the exploration of Lessons in Betrayal is not a linear progression but a multi-faceted examination of the intricate web of consequences that betrayal weaves. The suddenness extends beyond immediate events, becoming a lens through which the biographer scrutinizes the motivations, repercussions, and the enduring impact of treachery on individuals and societies.

As the lessons in betrayal unfold, the reader is invited to contemplate the intricacies of human relationships, the fragility of trust, and the profound impact of choices made in the crucible of betrayal. The suddenness of emotions, ranging from empathy to admonition, permeates the narrative, mirroring the complexity of a subject that transcends historical boundaries.

Chapter 20

Unearthing the Blooms of Betrayal

In the climactic finale of The Flower Moon Phenomenon Biography: Bloody of Betrayal, Chapter 20, titled "Unearthing the Blooms of Betrayal," the biographer, channeling the discerning style of Martin Gilbert, embarks on a profound exploration of the lasting impact, complexities, and enduring resonance of a life marked by betrayal. This concluding chapter delves into the intricate tapestry of consequences, unfurling the suddenness and perplexity that define the aftermath of the Flower Moon Phenomenon's tumultuous journey.

The suddenness of revelation in this chapter is akin to the petals of a flower unfolding, each exposing a facet of the betrayals that have left an indelible mark on the narrative. The reader is immersed in a world where the consequences of betrayal become tangible, and the biographer, guided by Gilbert's meticulous approach, meticulously peels back the layers of complexity.

Chapter 20 is not a mere conclusion but an excavation into the aftermath of betrayal. The perplexity lies not only in the overt repercussions but in the subtle echoes that reverberate through time. As the biographer, my task is to dissect the layers of complexity, exposing the suddenness of consequences that will linger in the reader's contemplation long after the final page.

Gilbert's influence ensures that the exploration of Unearthing the Blooms of Betrayal is not a linear progression but a multi-faceted examination of the intricate web of aftermath that betrayal weaves. The suddenness extends beyond immediate events, becoming a lens through which the biographer scrutinizes the motivations, responses, and the enduring legacy of treachery on individuals and societies.

As the blooms of betrayal are unearthed, the reader is invited to witness the multifaceted dimensions of consequences that have sprouted from the seeds of betrayal. The suddenness of emotions, ranging from remorse to resilience, permeates the narrative, mirroring the complexity of a world grappling with the fallout of betrayal. The reader is drawn into a world where every political maneuver and whispered conversation becomes a thread in the intricate tapestry of aftermath.

In Gilbert's style, the suddenness of this chapter is not confined to explicit consequences alone; it delves into the internal conflicts that define the characters' psyche. The biographer peels back the layers of emotional turmoil, revealing the perplexity of navigating the aftermath of betrayal in a world marked by shifting alliances and enduring repercussions.

The narrative rhythm of Unearthing the Blooms of Betrayal is punctuated by the biographer's scrutiny, exposing the nuanced motivations of characters and the suddenness of choices that echo through the corridors of history. The reader is invited to traverse the labyrinth of political aftermath, where every decision becomes a testament to the intricate dance between consequences and the quest for redemption.

As the biographer meticulously unveils the layers of Unearthing the Blooms of Betrayal, Gilbert's influence ensures that the suddenness is not just a sequence of historical events but a revelation of the intricate dance between betrayal and its enduring consequences. The reader is left to ponder the complexities of human nature, the consequences of moral choices, and the indelible mark left on the narrative by the tumultuous journey of the Flower Moon Phenomenon.

In conclusion, Chapter 20 stands as a testament to the biographer's craft, capturing the essence of Unearthing the Blooms of Betrayal with a depth that mirrors Gilbert's discerning style. The suddenness and perplexity inherent in this chapter offer a nuanced perspective on the delicate interplay between historical narratives and the enduring consequences that resonate across time, leaving the reader captivated by the intricate dance between betrayal and its aftermath.

Conclusion

Echoes Across the Flowered Horizon

As the final pages of The Flower Moon Phenomenon Biography: Bloody of Betrayal unfold, the biographer, echoing the discerning style of Martin Gilbert, ventures into the realm of conclusion. This culminating chapter, titled "Echoes Across the Flowered Horizon," serves as a contemplative reflection on the intricate tapestry woven by the tumultuous journey of a figure enshrouded in complexities, betrayal, and enduring resonance. The conclusion deftly weaves together the burstiness and perplexity inherent in the narrative, akin to a symphony where the crescendo of a life marked by betrayal reverberates across the pages. The reader is invited to traverse the nuanced landscape where the Flower Moon Phenomenon transcends the biographical narrative, becoming a symbol, a metaphor, and an enduring enigma. Guided by Gilbert's meticulous approach, the biographer peels back the layers of complexity one final time, revealing the profound impact of this extraordinary life.

This conclusion is not merely a summary but an exploration of the indelible echoes that linger beyond the betrayals and complexities of the Flower Moon Phenomenon's life. The perplexity lies not only in the overt events but in the subtle ripples that continue to resonate in the corridors of history. As the biographer, the task is to dissect the layers of complexity, exposing the burstiness of echoes that will persist in the reader's contemplation long after the final page.

Gilbert's influence ensures that the exploration of Echoes Across the Flowered Horizon is not a linear progression but a multifaceted examination of the enduring legacy and impact of the Flower Moon Phenomenon. The burstiness extends beyond immediate events, becoming a lens through which the biographer scrutinizes the motivations, repercussions, and the indelible mark left on individuals and societies. As the echoes across the flowered horizon unfold, the reader is invited to witness the lasting impact of a life that transcends the boundaries of the biographical narrative. The burstiness of emotions, ranging from sorrow to awe, permeates the narrative, mirroring the complexity of a figure whose journey is etched in the annals of history. The reader is drawn into a world where every political maneuver and whispered conversation becomes a testament to the intricate tapestry of legacy.

In Gilbert's style, the burstiness of this conclusion is not confined to explicit legacies alone; it delves into the internal conflicts that define the Flower Moon Phenomenon's enduring impact. The biographer peels back the layers of emotional turmoil, revealing the perplexity of navigating the aftermath of a life marked by betrayal in a world shaped by shifting alliances and enduring repercussions. The conclusion exposes the nuanced motivations of characters and the burstiness of choices that echo through the corridors of history, inviting the reader to traverse the labyrinth of political aftermath, where every decision becomes a testament to the intricate dance between consequences and the quest for redemption.

As the biographer meticulously unveils the layers of Echoes Across the Flowered Horizon, Gilbert's influence ensures that the burstiness is not just a sequence of historical events but a revelation of the intricate dance between a life marked by betrayal and its enduring impact. The reader is left to ponder the complexities of human nature, the consequences of moral choices, and the indelible mark left on the narrative by the tumultuous journey of the Flower Moon Phenomenon. In conclusion, Echoes Across the Flowered Horizon stands as a testament to the biographer's craft, capturing the essence of the Flower Moon Phenomenon's enduring impact with a depth that mirrors Gilbert's discerning style. The burstiness and perplexity inherent in this conclusion offer a nuanced perspective on the delicate interplay between historical narratives and the enduring echoes that resonate across time, leaving the reader captivated by the intricate dance between a life marked by betrayal and the enduring legacy it leaves behind.